FOSS Science

Water

Developed at

Lawrence Hall of Science

University of California at Berkeley

Published and Distributed by **Delta Education**

ISBN-10: 1-58356-842-5
ISBN-13: 978-1-58356-842-2
542-2014

6 7 8 9 10 11 QUE 12 11 10 09 08 07

TABLE OF CONTENTS

A REPORT FROM THE BLUE PLANET

TO: Chief of Science, Home Planet
FROM: Interplanetary Science Officer, Fleet 1138

Greetings from the blue planet I mentioned in my last report! I have been exploring it, as directed. Finally I know why it appears blue from space. Almost three-quarters of it is covered with water! (For your records, sir, pure water is a liquid with no smell and no taste.)

Ninety-seven percent of the planet's water is in its oceans. This is sea water, which is salty. A little more than two percent of the planet's water is frozen. This water forms glaciers and ice at the planet's poles. That leaves just one percent as usable fresh water. Much of that is underground. The rest is found on the surface. The people of the blue planet use this water. They drink it and cook with it. They use it for washing.

Water is matter. I have observed water in three states on the planet. It is found as liquid, ice, and vapor. Water is the only material on this planet found naturally in three different states. It occurs as a liquid, a solid, and a gas.

I encountered water first as a liquid. Drops of water hit our spaceship near the planet's surface. A new vocabulary word, sir: *rain.* This rain, along with my ship, landed in a *river.* The ship flowed into a larger body of water, or *lake.* (Another interesting fact is that water changes its shape! It takes the form of whatever container holds it!)

From the lake, the ship went over a *waterfall.* (See Damage Report 1.) The river below the waterfall carried the ship to an *ocean.*

An ocean current took the ship to a cold region. Some of the water was solid. An *ice* sheet covered the shore. Frozen water fell from the sky as *snow.* (Water can also freeze into *hail* and *sleet.*) Soon frozen water covered the ship windows as *frost.* I could not see anything outside. This led me to find another form of solid water. It's called an *iceberg.* (See Damage Report 2.)

At this point, we took off in our spaceship and flew through the planet's atmosphere. The snow and frost on the ship melted into water and then disappeared. As we flew through the atmosphere, we encountered puffy white formations called *clouds.* Closer inspection showed that clouds are made of tiny drops of water. We watched the droplets join together to form bigger drops, and then they fell toward the planet's surface. This is the rain I mentioned earlier in my report.

As you can see, sir, water is an amazing thing. In fact, I have discovered that it is vital. All living things here contain water. Even the bodies of the blue planet people are two-thirds water. Without water, life could not exist on the blue planet!

DAMAGE REPORT 1

Crumpled F-2000 panel on Sub-deck 3

Missing heat shield tiles

Damage sustained in plunge over a waterfall, water tumbling over a cliff.

DAMAGE REPORT 2

Shattered lens on front port external camera

Cracked plubium tube

Short circuit in guidance system circuit board

Damage sustained in collision with an iceberg, a massive block of frozen water floating in the ocean.

SURFACE TENSION

Have you ever seen an insect walk on water? If you have, you may have wondered how it could do that.

Water forms a "skin" where it meets the air. Water molecules on the surface are attracted to one another and form a surface like an elastic skin. That's *surface tension*. Insects such as water striders can walk on water because bristles on their feet keep them from breaking through the surface tension.

You can see how surface tension works. Fill a glass to the top with water. Keep adding more water a little at a time. If you are careful, you can "overfill" the glass. The water bulges up above the top of the glass, but it doesn't spill out.

In a rainstorm, a wet tent can keep you dry. Surface tension holds back the water. But don't touch the tent, or you'll break the surface tension!

Without surface tension, rain hitting a window would spread into a thin film. Instead the water forms beads.

Remember surface tension the next time you watch water striders zip across the water. The little insects glide over water as if they were skating on ice, thanks to surface tension.

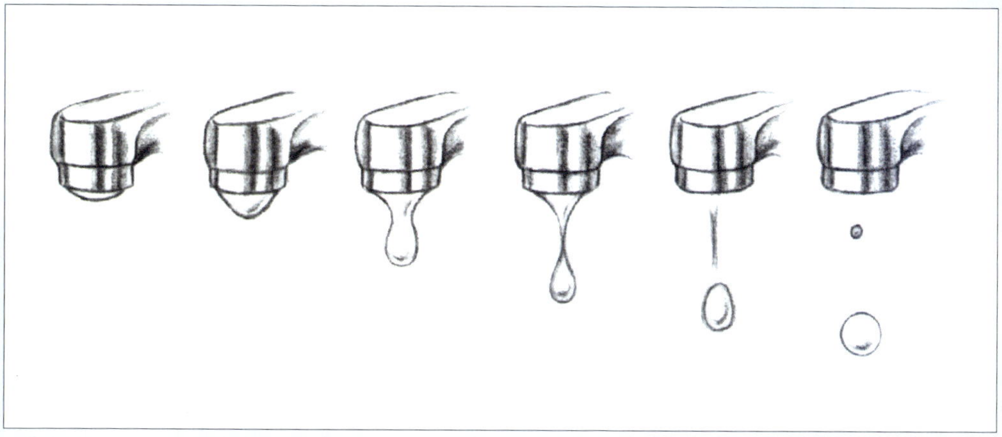

Surface tension is the property of water that causes it to form into a sphere.

WHICH WAY DOES IT GO?

Look out your window after a rainstorm. What happens to the rainwater? Some of it soaks down into the soil. Some of it runs along the top of the ground and on sidewalks and other paved surfaces. Because of gravity, all water always flows downward.

Melted snow flows down the sides of mountains and forms brooks. Brooks join to form streams, and streams tumble over cliffs as waterfalls.

Water moves very fast where the slope of land is steep, and it slows where the slope of land is gentle. Lakes and ponds form when water is surrounded by higher land. But water doesn't stay still. It always moves to lower ground.

THE POND

It's a warm summer day. A water flea swims along by moving its antennae, stopping every so often to feed on tiny algae. Then it's gone! It has been eaten by a small fish. The fish is hunted, too. A heron peers into the water, waiting for a chance to snap the fish up with its long beak. The fish hides in some underwater weeds.

This drama takes place in a small New York pond. The pond is shallow enough for sunlight to reach the bottom. The water hardly flows. The pond is home to many forms of life.

The pond is fed by water seeping from the ground. It gets more water from rain and melting snow. Sunlight is important here, because green plants and algae in the pond use sunlight to make food.

Most of the organisms in the pond are tiny. Algae do not have roots or leaves, so they float in the water. Some algae look like dots, while others are long strings of connected cells. Some plants such as duckweed float on the pond surface, too. Algae and plants are food for pond animals.

Underwater, weeds grow like trees in a forest. They shelter animals and put oxygen into the pond. On a summer day, small bubbles cover underwater plants. These dissolve into the water, providing oxygen for pond animals.

Rooted plants grow from shore to shore because the pond isn't deep. Tiny roots anchor water lilies in the mud. Water lilies don't need strong stems because they are supported by the water. Their floating leaves are called *pads.* Bigger plants like reeds and cattails grow at the edge of the pond. Dead plants are eaten by pond snails. This helps recycle the materials in the pond.

All summer, water striders walk across the pond's surface. They eat mosquito larvae trapped on the top of the surface film. Fish and tadpoles in the water eat algae and grow fat. They avoid hungry dragonfly nymphs. These young insects are hunters. They move through the water like jets by filling their abdomens with water, then forcing it out in powerful streams.

By the fall, many larvae have developed into adult insects. But dragonfly nymphs live in the water for several years, so many of them continue to prowl the pond. The tadpoles have become frogs by the time colder weather begins. Frogs and flying insects move away from the pond. Leaves from nearby trees blow onto the water. The days are shorter now, and nights are chilly. Life in the pond slows down. Some geese drop in late in the day, resting on a journey south. They spend the night, eating the duckweed and other plants.

In winter, the tree leaves sink to the pond bottom. They lie on the mud, providing shelter for diving beetles and snails. The duckweed sinks, too. Under the mud, the cold weather slows the body functions of turtles as they hibernate.

Later ice forms on the pond, surrounding the water lilies. They look brown and ragged. The fish move deeper underwater. The fish eat snails, but fish don't need much food because they are less active in winter. The dragonfly nymphs

are less active, too. A few plants under the ice get enough Sun to make food and oxygen. However, if the oxygen in the water falls to a low level, fish may crowd close to holes in the ice.

In the spring, duckweed plants float back to the surface, and soon they carpet the pond with green. Plants in the pond grow new leaves. On shore, reeds scatter their seeds. New shoots spring up from their roots.

Turtles emerge as days grow longer. Frogs return from damp grasses nearby. They lay eggs in the pond. Before long, tadpoles hatch. There are newborn snails and insects, too. The whole cycle of life in the pond begins again!

Ice Floats

Drop an ice cube into a glass of water, and the ice cube will float. That's because ice is less dense than water. And that's a good thing for water life!

When a pond or lake freezes, ice forms at the surface. It acts like a blanket. It keeps the deeper water from getting cold enough to freeze. That protects fish and other living things in the water.

If ice sank, the Sun's heat wouldn't reach it, and the ice wouldn't melt. Each year, more ice would form, and it would get deeper and deeper. Eventually the pond or lake would be a solid body of ice. Then all life in the water would die.

QUESTIONS TO EXPLORE

- **What are some of the plants and animals that live in the pond water?**
- **What are some of the animals that live both in and out of the pond water?**
- **What are some of the changes that take place in the pond throughout the year?**

ICE IS EVERYWHERE

Water changes from liquid to solid at 0°C (32°F). If temperatures drop to 0°C or lower, water becomes ice. In many areas, temperatures change with the seasons, and winter brings snow and ice. In the United States, northern areas such as New York, Illinois, and North Dakota have seasonal snow. Places such as Syracuse, New York, may have 2.8 meters (9.2 feet) of snow a year.

Some places are cold all year long. In the north, parts of Alaska, Greenland, Iceland, and Canada have ice year-round. But Antarctica, covering the South Pole, is the coldest continent. More than 95 percent of its land lies under ice. This ice cover is very thick. In some places, it can be 4,300 meters (14,200 feet) thick. In the winter, frozen sea water around Antarctica doubles the continent's size!

Sometimes in cold regions around the world, more snow falls than can be melted in the summer. The snow piles up and packs down into ice as it gets deeper. When the ice is about 18 meters (60 feet) thick, it begins to move across the land. Flowing ice is called a *glacier.* Glaciers are "rivers" of ice that gravity moves downhill.

Scientists keep track of how far glaciers move. An average glacier advances less than 1 meter (3.3 feet) each day. Glaciers in Iceland and Alaska have been recorded at speeds of more than 100 meters (330 feet) per day.

Glaciers now cover almost ten percent of the Earth. They are found in

Mount Kilimanjaro

Where Do Icebergs Come From?

Are icebergs made of fresh water or salt water?

Icebergs are drifting "islands" of ice. They may look white, green, or blue. They're found in the ocean but are not made of salt water. Icebergs are frozen fresh water. Have you ever wondered where they come from?

Icebergs were once parts of glaciers. When a glacier reaches the sea, pieces at the end break off. These chunks of ice may be as small as a meter or many kilometers long. The largest ever measured was 320 kilometers (200 miles) long and 96 kilometers (60 miles) wide!

We see only a small part of an iceberg. Seven-eighths is hidden beneath the water's surface. Icebergs in the North Atlantic last up to 2 years before melting, depending on their size. Icebergs in the Antarctic are often much larger, and they may last up to 10 years.

During World War II (1939–1945), the Allies considered using an iceberg as an airfield! Some years later, one iceberg in the Arctic Ocean was put to use. "Fletcher's Ice Island" was set up as a research station in March 1952. It was used several times in the 1950s and 1960s.

Someday icebergs may be a useful source of fresh water. Ice could be "harvested" and melted. Whole icebergs might even be towed to countries needing fresh water!

all the major mountain ranges. They exist on every continent except Australia. All the glaciers in the world store about 75 percent of the world's fresh water. If they melted, sea level would rise about 79 meters (260 feet).

Sometimes snow and ice form where you wouldn't expect them. In 1848, two Germans brought a story home from Africa. They reported seeing a snow-covered mountain near the equator. At first, no one believed them. Wasn't every place at the equator too warm for snow?

The Germans had seen Kilimanjaro, the tallest mountain in Africa. It rises to 5,895 meters (19,340 feet). All year long, Kilimanjaro is capped with ice. That's because temperature decreases with altitude. The higher you travel, the colder the air becomes. Snow and ice can exist anywhere temperatures are low enough, even at the equator!

ICE HISTORY

Workers use a horse and sled to mark the frozen surface of a lake.

Workers cut sheets of ice that are floated to an icehouse.

Imagine if refrigerators had never been invented. How would we keep milk and other food from spoiling?

Before refrigeration, people used ice to keep food cool. Around the beginning of the 20th century, ice used to be "harvested" wherever lakes and rivers froze in wintertime. People waited until the ice was at least 60 centimeters (2 feet) thick. It needed to be strong enough to hold the ice workers.

Horses were harnessed and driven onto the ice. They wore spiked horseshoes so they wouldn't slip. They plowed the frozen lake or river like a field to clear away any snow. Then the horses pulled a special tool that scratched lines in the ice. First lines were drawn in one direction, and then those lines were crossed with others to make a pattern of pieces for cutting.

Then the ice was ready to be cut. Workers used sharp saws and followed the lines on the ice. Soon blocks of ice floated on the water, and these were pushed with poles to icehouses.

Igloos

Igloo is the word for "house" in the Inuit people's language. Some Canadian Inuit build snow igloos when they are on long journeys. They pile blocks of snow into a dome shape. The entrance to the igloo is long and low. Inuit crawl inside on their hands and knees. The snow house protects them from cold winds.

Icehouses looked like barns. Inside, the ice blocks were carefully stacked and stored. Straw or sawdust was spread over and around each one to keep the ice from melting and sticking to other ice blocks.

Throughout the year, ice was taken from the icehouse. Horse-drawn trucks carried blocks of it to towns and cities. Children loved to see the ice truck on hot summer days. They ran after it until it stopped. Canvas flaps on the truck kept the ice shaded and cool. The children stayed close when the iceman pushed a flap aside. How good the cold air felt!

The iceman wore leather shoulder pads and a leather apron. These kept him from getting wet and cold. He used ice tongs to grab the blocks, and he carried the ice on his shoulder. The ice blocks might weigh from 11 to 22 kilograms (25 to 50 pounds) each.

The iceman chipped at the block with an ice pick. The ice was cut and shaped to fit inside an icebox. The icebox was the place where the ice kept food cool. Most homes had an icebox. Children gathered around to watch the iceman do his work. There was sure to be a sliver of ice for each of them. What a treat on a steamy day!

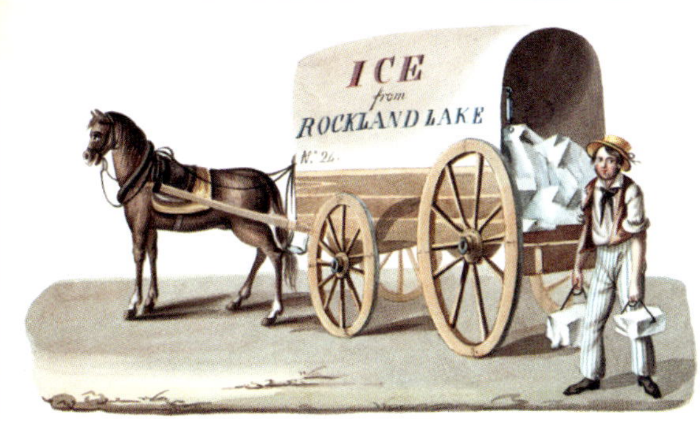

Why Pipes Burst

Pipes supply water to houses, schools, and other buildings. They may be made of plastic, copper, cast iron, steel, or other materials. They're made to be strong, but sometimes pipes burst! Do you know why?

Most things *contract,* or grow smaller, when they get cold. Water shrinks as it cools, too. But when water gets down to 4°C (39°F), it starts to expand. The colder it gets, the more it expands, until it freezes. That means ice takes up more space than liquid water does. Ice needs room to expand, or it will break its container.

In places where temperatures drop below freezing, care must be taken to keep water from freezing in pipes. Pipes should be wrapped with insulation. Heating systems can keep areas with pipes warm. Sometimes unused water pipes can be drained of water before the cold season begins.

A Soggy Mass

Water played an important role in developing the metric system. It was used to set the standard for the *gram.* The gram is the metric unit of mass. The gram is equal to 1 cubic centimeter of pure water at 4°C. At that temperature, water is densest. That means its molecules are most tightly packed.

The wettest place on Earth

The driest place on Earth

WET AND DRY PLACES

Scientists who study the climate keep track of *precipitation*, which is how much rain and snow falls. Over the last 100 years, the United States averaged about 73 centimeters (29 inches) of precipitation a year. Some parts of the country had a lot of rain, while others had very little. Precipitation doesn't fall in equal amounts all over the world. The amount of rain a place gets depends on many things. Some factors are wind, the shape of the land, and its geographic location.

The wettest place on Earth is Mount Waialeale in Hawaii. Over a 30-year period, rainfall there averaged 1,168 centimeters (460 inches) a year!

Compare that to the Atacama Desert in Chile. It gets about three-quarters of a millimeter (0.03 inches) of rain each year. That makes it the driest place in the world. Some years, the Atacama Desert gets no rain at all. It holds the world's record for the longest rainless period. It had no rain from October 1903 to January 1918, a span of over 14 years!

Deserts have slow water cycles. Any water vapor in the air cannot condense. That is one reason why deserts get very little rain.

Tropical rainforests usually get more than 250 centimeters (100 inches) of rain a year. Many plants add water vapor to the air. Before long, the air cannot hold any more water, and rain falls hard. The water cycle in a rainforest is fast.

EVAPORATION AND CONDENSATION

Sometimes water seems mysterious. Wipe a chalkboard with a wet sponge, and the water left behind quickly vanishes! Take a hot shower, and water appears on the mirror out of thin air! How do these things happen?

Water is always changing from one state to another. When you wipe a chalkboard, liquid water left behind escapes into the air, becoming water vapor. The same thing happens to water splashed onto a counter. Left alone, it soon disappears. We call this change from a liquid to a gas *evaporation*. Evaporation happens around you every day. Sometimes you depend on it! Evaporation dries your clothes after you come out of the rain.

When you take a hot shower, some water changes into water vapor. But when it touches a mirror's cool surface, the vapor turns back into liquid water. When water vapor becomes liquid water, this change is called *condensation*. Condensation is the reason a cold drink "sweats." The air and the water vapor in the air are warmer than the cold drink. Water vapor from the air hits the cool glass, which cools the vapor and turns it into liquid water. The water collects on the outside of the glass.

Condensation on a window

Did you ever wonder why you can see your breath on a cold day? That's condensation, too. Cold air cools the water vapor in your breath. The cloud you see is made of tiny water droplets.

THE WATER CYCLE

The amount of water on Earth is fairly constant. We use it over and over again. It's *recycled.* Water you swallow today may have once rained into the Grand Canyon. It may have washed one of Abraham Lincoln's shirts. It might even have been a dinosaur's drink!

Energy from the Sun changes water. It turns liquid water into a gas called *water vapor.* This change is called *evaporation.* You don't see water vapor because it's invisible. Water evaporates from lakes, rivers, and oceans. It evaporates from puddles and clothes hung on a line.

Warm air carries water vapor up into the sky. Air carries water from one place to another. As air rises, it cools, and water vapor in the air cools, too. When that happens, water vapor changes into liquid water, and tiny droplets form. This change from water vapor to liquid water is called *condensation.*

Moist air that cools near the ground forms *dew.* Dew is made of water droplets that condense on surfaces such as blades of grass and leaves. *Frost* forms when water vapor becomes ice directly on a surface that is 0°C (32°F) or colder.

Higher in the air, water droplets form around tiny pieces of dust. At first, each droplet is too small to see. But droplets bump into each other and join together, and the droplets grow larger and larger. It takes millions of these clumps of water droplets to form *clouds.*

If it is cold, the water droplets may form ice crystals. The water droplets or ice crystals may get too heavy to stay in the air, so they fall to Earth as rain. Oceans cover more than 70 percent of the world, so most rain falls there.

On land, rain is taken in by plant roots. It escapes into the air through holes in plant leaves. Rain also lands on roofs and roads. Sunshine evaporates more than half the rain that falls. This water may move through the water cycle quickly.

Evaporation, condensation, precipitation, and the movement of water over and through the ground are all part of the water cycle.

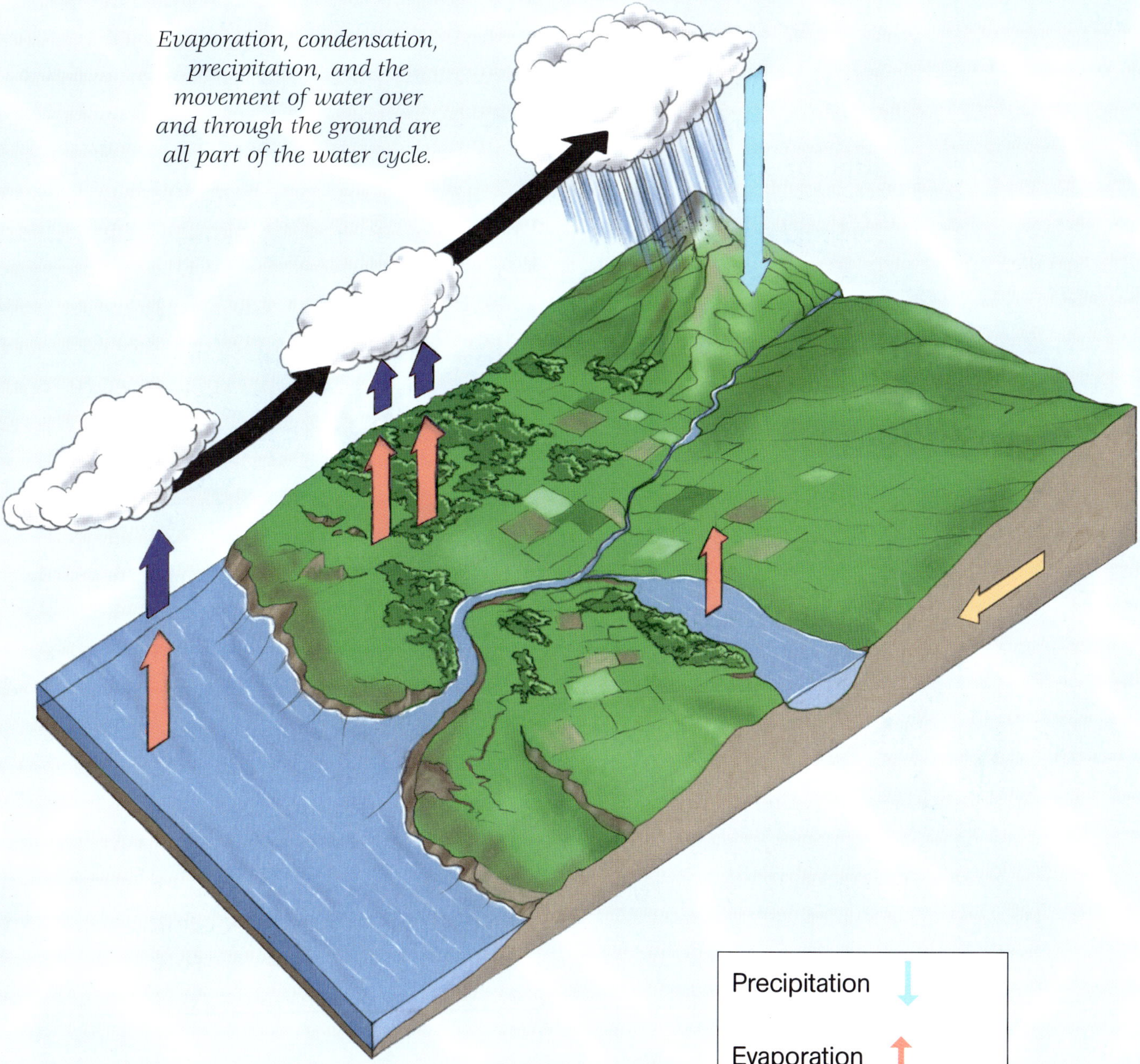

Ninety-seven percent (97%) of Earth's water is salt water in the oceans. Fresh water evaporates from the oceans. It condenses in the atmosphere, forming clouds. Oceans are the source of most of the water in the water cycle.

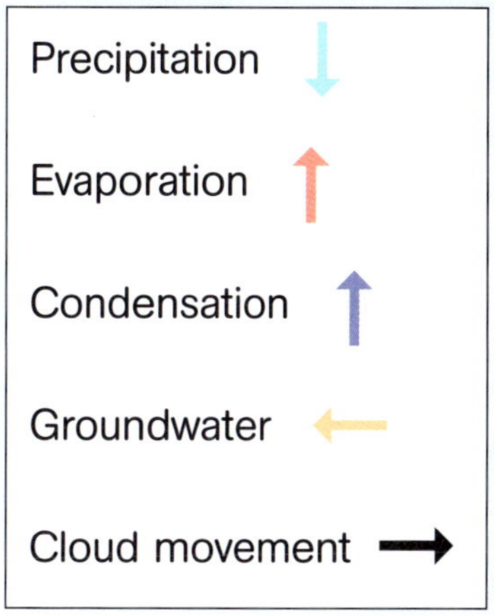

Some rainwater runs along the ground. The water drops might join a stream, and after a long journey, they may reach the ocean.

Other rain sinks into the ground. *Groundwater* finds the lowest pathway. It flows through sand and pebbles and may seep slowly through clay. Groundwater often moves slowly. It might take 100 years to emerge as a spring!

We pump some groundwater back to the surface, where it is purified and sent through pipes. Once purified, you might drink it, or you might wash your clothes in it. It might be flushed down a toilet. It could be a long time before it becomes water vapor again, or it could become vapor again quickly.

Ice sheets and glaciers take the longest time to go through the water cycle. Water may stay frozen for hundreds or even thousands of years! But all water is part of the same cycle that changes over and over. Water freezes into ice. Ice melts into water. Water becomes vapor. Vapor changes back into water. It happens every day. It's a never-ending cycle that supports life on Earth.

Ice crystals

QUESTIONS TO EXPLORE

- **How do drops of rain form?**
- **What's the difference between frost and dew?**
- **What causes water to evaporate? To condense?**

WATER

A Vital Resource

by Keira, David, Tamiko, and Jorge

Our team's assignment was to learn about our water supply. The Earth seems to have plenty of water. Nearly three-quarters of its surface is covered by water. But 97 percent of that water is in the oceans, and that means it's salty. We can't drink salt water. Another two percent of the world's water is frozen. That leaves just one percent as fresh water for use on our planet! The good news is that one percent should be enough for everyone. The bad news is that it's not spread equally around the world. Some places have a lot of fresh water, but others do not.

Tamiko brought some information to our first meeting. She said we use 35 times as much water today as people did 300 years ago. The population has grown and so have the ways we use water. She said, "More than half of the available fresh water is now being used by people."

Jorge looked surprised and asked, "Will we ever run out of water?"

Keira was sure the answer was no. She reminded us what we had learned about the water cycle. She said, "The amount of water on Earth stays pretty much the same. It gets recycled."

But David wondered if the amount of water we need could grow larger than the amount we have. That made all of us realize how important it is to take care of the water we have. Tamiko summed it up this way. "Water is one of the most vital resources on Earth!"

At the end of the meeting, each of us chose something to investigate about our water supply. We agreed we had a lot to learn!

Water Coming into Our Homes

by Keira

Our water is taken from Lake Charles. In other places, water comes from rivers or underground sources called *aquifers.* Aquifers contain rainwater that has soaked into the ground and is stored in a layer of rock or sediment. No matter where water is found, it is treated before it reaches our faucets. Water purification plants clean and treat the water, making it safe for people to use. Before water comes into our homes, it goes through many steps.

First water is screened to remove fish, leaves, and large objects such as logs or trash. Next a machine called a *flash mixer* stirs the water with chemicals. Four chemicals are commonly mixed with water. They are *lime, carbon, chlorine,* and *alum.* Lime softens the water. Carbon collects things in the water that smell bad. Chlorine kills bacteria. Alum makes small particles in the water clump together. These form larger particles that are heavy enough to sink.

A water filtration plant

The mixed water goes to a settling tank. Dirt, sand, and other particles drift to the bottom. From there, the water passes through a filter which has layers of sand, gravel, and charcoal. At this point, more chlorine is added. A chemist at the water treatment plant tests the water every day. This is to make sure that all harmful bacteria are killed. Purified water is pumped into tanks and towers. It reaches our homes through underground pipes.

Water Leaving Our Homes

by David

Water leaves our homes, too. It runs down sink and bathtub drains and out of washing machines. It is flushed down toilets. Waste water must be treated before it reenters the water system. In some communities, waste water goes to sewage treatment plants. In other places, waste water enters septic systems.

Septic tanks are usually made of concrete or metal. They are buried underground outside houses. Waste water in a septic tank separates. Heavy solids sink to the bottom and form *sludge.* Lighter solids like fats and grease rise and form *scum.* The layer in the middle flows through pipes into gravel-filled trenches. Solids in the tank are broken down by bacteria. They slowly *decompose,* or break down. The liquid in the trenches is purified as it seeps through the gravel and soil.

A concrete septic tank being installed

At sewage treatment plants, waste water is screened to remove solids. Other materials are broken down by bacteria. Chemicals are used to rid the water of impurities. Treated water is then discharged into streams, lakes, or the ocean.

Runoff

by Tamiko

Rain that does not evaporate or soak into the ground becomes *runoff.* Runoff flows through streets and into storm drains. These drains often empty right into bays, lakes, and streams. Since this water is not treated, it can do immediate harm to the water supply. Pet waste must never be dumped into storm drains. In addition, we must be careful how we dispose of oils, paints, and hazardous products. They cannot be poured into storm drains or onto driveways or streets because rain will carry them into the water supply. In some places, science clubs or environmental groups paint pictures of fish on the sidewalks near storm drains. The fish remind people that whatever goes into the storm drain will enter our water supply!

Water Conservation

by Jorge

Conserving water is an important part of protecting it. Because of conservation efforts in the United States, water use has dropped since 1980. Here are a few things we can do to save water.

- ☺ Water left running wastes hundreds of liters of water. Turn off the tap when you brush your teeth. Don't run water while washing dishes. Shut the shower off while you soap up.
- ☺ Take shorter showers and use a "low-flow" shower head.
- ☺ Install "low-flow" aerators on all your faucets. An aerator mixes air with the water. You use less water when air is mixed in. The flow will still seem strong.
- ☺ Fix any leaks in pipes or faucets.
- ☺ Use less water to flush your toilet. Put a water-filled plastic container in the tank.
- ☺ Use a broom to clean your driveway instead of using the hose.
- ☺ Water your lawn in the morning. Water evaporates faster in the middle of the day. Don't water on a windy day. Aim the water carefully, and don't sprinkle the street.
- ☺ Use mulch around plants to reduce evaporation.

QUESTIONS TO EXPLORE

- What is the source of your local water?
- How is water purified in your community? How is sewage treated in your community?
- What are the issues about water in your community?

THE POWER OF WATER

A flood destroys homes.

Water does more than support life on Earth. Flowing water is powerful. This power is used in many positive ways. But sometimes water causes problems.

Storms add water to rivers and streams. Water flows faster as river and stream levels rise. Floods occur when rivers or streams overflow their banks. Floodwaters carry away soil, and they damage property and roadways. The faster water flows, the more it can carry. Swiftly moving water can carry away cars or even houses!

Strong rain may cause water to rise rapidly. *Flash floods* and *mudslides* come without warning. Mudslides happen when soil on sloping ground contains too much water. Mudslides have destroyed whole villages in some mountain areas.

Hurricanes cause storm surges.

Hurricanes are responsible for most coastal flooding. These storms damage property and may leave people homeless. Rain and strong winds near the coast cause *storm surges.* Ocean waves grow higher and pound shorelines.

Undersea earthquakes send waves moving under the ocean. These waves are called *tsunamis.* They travel up to 800 kilometers (500 miles) an hour! Tsunamis grow higher as they near shore. They can often grow to 30 meters (100 feet) high before they strike land. A 60-meter

(200-foot) tsunami hit Lituya Bay, Alaska, in 1958. It destroyed trees as high as 520 meters (1,700 feet) above sea level!

Some people think we shouldn't build in places where water levels rise. Others want to live near the water. They are willing to risk floods and wave damage to live by the water.

Egyptians channeled water for *irrigation* as early as 5000 B.C.E. Irrigation systems are used today in dry places, supplying moisture needed by crops. Dams may be built to store water for irrigation. The water is transported to plants through canals. Sometimes water is sprinkled or dripped onto plants. Irrigation increases the amount of food grown worldwide.

Hoover Dam

Wheels turned by flowing water can do work. Waterwheels have been used for thousands of years. The early Greeks and Romans used them to grind corn. Early American towns used waterwheels to power gristmills and sawmills.

Heated water creates steam. Steam expanding in a closed space can power engines. The steam engine led to advances in transportation and industry. Steam soon was used to run carriages and riverboats. Pumps, factories, and mills were all powered by steam.

Hydroelectric plants use the power of water to make electricity. Water flows through large rotary engines called *turbines.* Turbines have wheels with paddles, blades, or buckets. They are pushed by flowing water. The moving wheels turn *drive shafts.* The drive shafts power machines such as electric generators. Today hydropower produces about one-quarter of the world's energy!

ELLEN SWALLOW RICHARDS:
AN EARLY ECOLOGIST

An American in 1900 could expect to live only to age 47. Today life expectancy is much greater. We owe that in part to Ellen Swallow Richards. She lived in a time when people understood little about germs and pollution. Yet Richards knew there was a connection between health and the environment. In the early 1900s, she wrote to the president of the Massachusetts Institute of Technology (MIT), "One of the most serious problems of civilization is clean water and clean air, not only for ourselves but for the world."

Ellen Swallow was born on December 3, 1842. She lived in Dunstable, Massachusetts. Growing up, Ellen did chores on the family's farm and helped in their store. She also took care of her mother, who was often sick. Ellen's first teachers were her parents. They saw that Ellen loved to learn. Before long, they moved the family to Westford, Massachusetts, where Ellen entered school.

Richards in her study

Ellen became a teacher after graduation, but soon her mother was sick again. Ellen returned home to help out, but she was unhappy working in the family store. She wanted to learn more, and she wanted to go to college.

Few colleges accepted women at that time. Many people believed studying hard would make women ill! But Ellen would not forget her dream. She worked at many jobs and saved all the money she could. Finally she had enough money to enter Vassar College. Vassar was an experimental school. It aimed to give women the same chance men had to get an education.

Ellen was called a "special student" at Vassar because she was 26 years old. The other women were much younger. Their ages ranged from 14 to 19. Ellen was too happy to care. Her favorite subjects were astronomy and chemistry. In 1870, she was part of Vassar's first graduating class.

Ellen planned to teach in Argentina, but war broke out there. She became a graduate student at MIT instead. She didn't pay tuition there. Ellen believed this was because she was poor. In fact, MIT was afraid to admit women. By not charging Ellen, the school could claim she was not really a student!

Ellen worked at MIT after her graduation in 1873. The professors respected her. One laboratory head said, "When we are in doubt about anything we always go to Miss Swallow." Ellen married chemistry professor Robert H. Richards in 1875. They helped each other with their work.

In 1884, Ellen Swallow Richards was made an instructor of "sanitary chemistry." For 2 years, she and Professor Thomas M. Drown studied the state's water supply. They suspected that something in the water was making people sick. Richards worked to find a way to test the water quality. Water was collected from every river and lake in Massachusetts once a month. Richards analyzed most of the 40,000 samples herself. When the survey was done, Massachusetts had the first standard for water purity. Dr. Drown wrote that this was "mainly due to Mrs. Richards' great zeal and vigilance." From then on, Richards taught others how to analyze air, water, and sewage.

The MIT Chemistry Department in 1900

Ellen Swallow Richards was a pioneer. She started the Women's Laboratory at MIT in 1876. She wanted other women to study science. When the Women's Laboratory closed in 1883, Richards was thrilled. Through her efforts, women were no longer "special" at MIT. They were regular students, just like the men.

Another of Richards's interests was nutrition. She opened the New England Kitchen, where immigrants were taught how to cook nutritious, inexpensive food. She cared deeply about public health. She urged women to eat right and exercise.

Ellen Swallow Richards died of a heart attack on March 30, 1911. Many people consider her to be the founder of ecology. She said, "The quality of life depends on the ability of society to teach its members how to live in harmony with their environment...." It was Richards's belief that science should make people healthier. She worked hard to make that happen.

MOON DREAMS

For a long time, I had two dreams. One was to get a dog, and the other was to see the Apollo astronauts' footprints on the Moon.

"It should be a big, friendly dog," I told my mom. "I want it to follow me around and sleep at the end of my bed."

But Mom didn't think that dream could come true. She said, "Brad, you know how much it costs to send us anything. We get only what is needed."

"Then how about seeing the footprints?" I asked.

I used to think it would be easy. After all, my parents are lunar engineers, and we live on the Moon! It wasn't, though. And not because Neil Armstrong took that first "small step" in 1969, which was over 100 years ago. His footprints will last a million years because there's no air or wind here to blow the dirt around. The real reason was that we're not near those early landing sites. And it doesn't seem like I'll get close to them anytime soon. My family's been here 3 years so far, and I still haven't stepped on the outside surface of the Moon!

Our colony is in a lunar crater, which is covered by a bubble and a water shield. The water shield blocks harmful rays from the Sun and helps control the colony's temperature. Pipes circulate the water between sunlight and darkness. I don't spend much time under the bubble, though. Most of the colony is underground. I use Corridor 12 to go between home and school. I hardly ever see the stars.

School is where I learned about the Apollo missions. Those early astronauts knew so little about the Moon. They didn't even know there was water here. Dad always reminds me we aren't living on the Moon because of the Apollo astronauts. He says we should thank the Lunar Prospector spacecraft. Back in 1998, it confirmed water frozen around the Moon's poles. We mine that ice. "Without it," Dad says, "it would be too hard to live on the Moon."

"Absolutely," Mom always adds. "It would be much too expensive to ship all of our water here."

I never thought about water until I moved here. It's amazing how Earth uses the same water over and over. We have recycling on the Moon, too. It's our own miniature water cycle! There's no weather, of course, so we don't have clouds dropping snow or rain. But water vapor in our air condenses on the cool water pipes. That pure water is collected. Our waste water is collected, too. It's heated at high pressure, and the waste is burned away. Pure water is left, along with compounds used for fertilizer.

Everybody in the colony thinks about how we use water. We know it's much too precious to waste. We need water to survive, and so do the plants we grow for food. But the Moon's water has even more uses. We break it down with solar-powered electricity. It turns into hydrogen and oxygen. That makes our air. It also is used for rocket fuel! I can understand why Dad calls water a hero.

Still, the Apollo astronauts were heroes to me, too. They were brave to travel so far from Earth. That's why I was excited when Mom and Dad started to hint that one of my dreams might come true! When they took me to the spaceport, I was sure I was about to see those ancient footprints!

A shuttle had just landed. A conveyer belt in the tube connecting the shuttle to the spaceport carried new supplies.

"Come on!" I said. "Let's put on suits! I can't wait to see the footprints!"

"Not so fast," Mom said. "One of these packages might be for us."

Sure enough, a small refrigerated container was marked with our name.

"What's in there?" I asked.

"A petri dish," Dad said.

I was confused.

Mom smiled at Dad, then she smiled at me. "It would be too expensive to send a dog to the Moon," she said, "so we're going to grow one of our own!"

They'd had a dog's cells sent to the Moon in the petri dish! I finally got my dog!

I have a new dream now. I still want to see the footprints. But I also want to teach my dog Neil not to jump up on people. The Moon's gravity is only one-sixth of Earth's, and when Neil gets excited, he springs almost 4 meters (13 feet) into the air!

GLOSSARY

Algae Any of a large group of mostly aquatic organisms that contain the green pigment chlorophyll but lack veins.

Condensation The process by which water vapor changes into liquid water, usually on a surface.

Cycle A process or action that repeats itself in the same order over time.

Dissolve To break down into particles so small when mixed with water that a substance seems to disappear.

Evaporation The process by which liquid water changes into water vapor.

Flash flood A sudden flow of water over the land. Flash floods usually occur within a few minutes or hours of excessive rainfall.

Freeze To change from a liquid to a solid state as a result of cooling.

Gas A state of a substance with no definite shape or volume; usually invisible.

Glacier A large mass of ice moving slowly over land.

Gravity The natural force that pulls objects toward each other. On Earth, all objects are pulled toward the center of the Earth.

Ice The solid state of water.

Iceberg A large mass of ice that has become detached from a glacier and floats in the ocean.

Liquid A state of a substance with no definite shape but a definite volume.

Matter Anything that has mass.

Melt To change from a solid to a liquid state as a result of warming.

Molecule The smallest part of a substance that is made up of two or more atoms.

Slope A slanted or tilted surface.

Solid A state of a substance with a definite shape and volume.

Storm surge Water pushed ahead of a storm like snow before a shovel. Water piles up along a coast, rushing toward land faster than it can return to the sea.

Surface tension The skinlike surface on water (and other liquids) that pulls it together into the smallest possible volume (a sphere).

Water A liquid earth material made of hydrogen and oxygen.

Water quality A term used to describe the purity of water.

Water vapor The gaseous state of water.